NATIONAL GEOGRAPHIC

Up the Amazon

Gare Thompson

Contents

The Amazon River

Let's travel the second longest river in the world. The Amazon River is about 4,000 miles (6,440 kilometers) long. It flows through many countries in South America.

Our trip will take us deep into the heart of the world's largest **rain forest**. Pack your camera and your binoculars. You don't want to miss taking photos of the wonderful sights we'll see.

It rains a lot where we are going. So bring rain gear and a waterproof sleeping bag. Pack light clothes. Most of the time the air is hot and humid. Light clothes will dry out faster. Ready? Let's go!

Amazing Facts

Around the Amazon you can find:

- The world's largest tropical rain forest.
- Hundreds of different kinds of mammals.
- Thousands of different kinds of freshwater fish.
- Tens of thousands of different kinds of trees.
- Millions of different kinds of insects.

Starting Out: Belém

A Museum Tour

We are in the city Belém, in Brazil. It is at the **mouth** of the mighty Amazon River. The mouth of a river is the place where the river empties into a large body of water. At Belém, the Amazon fans out to join the Atlantic Ocean.

You can see where the Amazon meets the Atlantic Ocean. No other river pours out as much water! There are more than 1,000 other rivers that flow into the Amazon. Some parts of the river run fast. The **currents** can be strong and dangerous.

Let's go into a museum. The museum has a zoo, a garden, and a research center. Here we will see and feel what the rain forest will be like.

Agouti

Inside the noise is loud. Insects called cicadas are making the noise. Our guide tells us that there are millions of different kinds of bugs in the rain forest. It's a good thing I like bugs.

I almost step on an agouti. It is a large rodent. Yuck! The guide reminds me that that I will have to watch where I walk, sit, and lean in the forest. I don't want to sit on a snake or scorpion!

We see a manatee. It is also called a sea cow. It swims in the water. We also see a harpy eagle. It is the strongest bird of prey in the world. It is amazing.

Manatee

The Harbor

Belém is a busy harbor city. We stop at the fish market.
You can find all kinds of fish here. The fish come from
the Amazon River. It has more kinds of fish living in it
than any other river. People sell piranha, a flesh-eating
fish. They also sell surubim, a long-nosed, striped catfish.
It is funny looking, but it tastes good. Walking around
the market is like being inside an aquarium.

People sell more than fish in the harbor. Boats deliver
all kinds of goods. There are tables of fruits that are
grown along the river. There are also birds for sale.

Piranha

Like other markets, pottery and clothes are also for sale. There are plants for sale, too. Many of the plants are used as medicine.

We will sail from Belém up the river. We'll sail about 1,000 miles (1,610 kilometers) to the next major city, Manaus. On the way we will stop and explore some of the **tributaries** that flow into the Amazon. Our guide says each river is like entering a different world.

Up the River

Our boat is a large cruise ship. My room is small. It has a small, round window. All you can see is the river. Because the boat is large, it feels like we are hardly moving.

The guide tells us more about the river. Some parts of the Amazon look brown and muddy. That's because the water is carrying soil, called **sediment**. The sediment makes the river looks brown.

Dolphins live in the Amazon. They are freshwater dolphins. These dolphins are born gray, but can turn pink as they get older. Finally, we see two. They are like a splash of pink paint against a dark canvas.

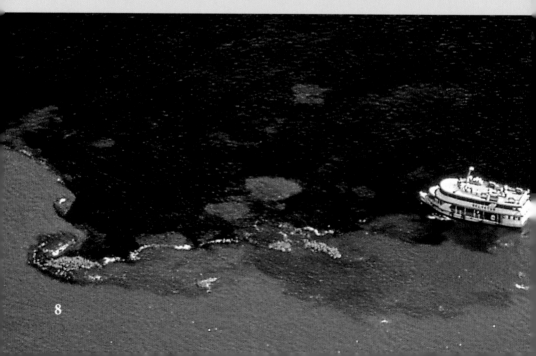

Basilisk

We stop to see some fishermen. They have caught an arapaima. This is one of the biggest freshwater fish in the world. It is almost 10 feet long (3 meters) and weighs over 200 pounds (90 kilograms). This fish feeds a lot of people! The local people eat it dried.

Later, we see a small lizard called a basilisk. I use my binoculars to look at it. It is close to shore. It runs across the water on its back legs. Its toes have flaps on them. It is funny to see the basilisk running across the water.

At night the river is noisy. The bugs, the birds, and the noise of the river itself finally lull me to sleep. It is still hot at night. We sleep with bug nets over our hammocks. The bugs do not seem to sleep.

Exploring a Small River

It is early morning. The sun is bright. It is hot and humid. Our guide tells us to bring our rain gear because it will rain later. It rains here almost every day. That is why many parts of the river are so deep. The river gets deeper during the rainy season. We leave the ship and travel in a small boat.

We take it up a small river that flows into the Amazon. The water moves faster in the smaller river than on the Amazon. The guide controls the boat. It is hard work.

Morpho butterfly

We find a spot to stop. The guide warns us to be alert as we explore. We must also stay together. The air is damp. After a few minutes we are all wet. My clothes squish as I walk.

Then I see a magical sight. It is a beautiful, blue butterfly called a morpho. Our guide tells us that airplane pilots see these amazing butterflies as they fly over the river. The butterfly shimmers in the light. It is like a flying jewel. It moves very fast. The guide says that they are easy to see, but very hard to catch. They live high in the trees.

Trees hang over us. The guide points out the many layers of plants in the forest. The plants fight for sunlight. Different birds and animals live at each layer. Suddenly a macaw swoops by. It looks like a flying rainbow. It is brightly colored. It has a powerful beak to break nuts. It is the largest of all parrots.

We make our way back to the boat. I watch out for bugs. They seem to be everywhere.

Macaw

Amazing Facts

There's an ant in the rain forest called the "24 hour" ant. Its sting lasts for a full day.

Docking in Manaus

We dock at the **port** of Manaus in Brazil. The port is filled with boats. There are cruise ships filled with people. There are fishing boats full of fish. And there are boats filled with other kinds of goods. The Amazon is like a highway. But instead of cars and trucks, there are boats.

Our guide tells us about the city. In the 1890s, Manaus was the "king" of the rubber trade. Rubber trees grew around the city. There were many **plantations**, or large rubber farms. Ships carried the rubber down the Amazon.

By the early 1900s, Manaus was one of the richest cities in the Americas. Ships came to Manaus from all over the world. But then rubber production moved to the Far East. Many people left Manaus.

Today, tourists visit Manaus. People living here work in hotels and restaurants. Others sell goods to the tourists. After being on the boat so long, it is nice to be in a city and to sleep in a bed.

Manaus is on the bank of the Rio Negro. We decide to explore this river that runs into the Amazon. The Rio Negro is almost black. It is dark because the leaves in the river turn the water dark. They stain the water like tea.

Tapping rubber from a tree

Amazing Facts

Rubber was very important to Brazil. People could not take rubber seeds out of the country. But some seeds were stolen in 1876. They were planted in the Far East. Soon that area of the world became "king of rubber."

We see a fin break the water. It is a small river dolphin. We watch it surface two or three more times before it disappears. Then we hear birds screeching. We look up and see a huge flock of parakeets. They are very noisy birds.

In this shallow part, the river looks like a green carpet. The green carpet turns out to be huge water lilies. These water lilies are about 6 feet (2 meters) across! A small child can float on them! We finally get past them and spot more fish.

We see a school of red piranha. The guide tells us to keep our hands in the boat! These fish can tear a large animal to bits in minutes. I sit on my hands!

Slowly we make our way back to the city. We will make one more stop in our large ship. Then we have to travel by canoe. It is the only way to reach the **source,** or the beginning, of the Amazon River.

Water lilies

Visiting a River Village

We take the boat to Iquitos, Peru. The water is a little rougher than when we started out. Now we must travel by canoe. Parts of the river are not deep enough for big boats. In other places the river narrows and is filled with jagged rocks. We get into our canoe and wave goodbye to the people on the dock.

Amazing Facts

Long ago people used canoes, called dugouts, to travel the river. They hollowed out trees to make their canoes. Today, many villagers still use these canoes.

Now it seems like we are entering the heart of the river. The river flows faster here. The guide watches for rocks and narrow passages. It is easy to tip the canoe over in the fast **rapids**. We wear life jackets.

We are going deeper into the forest as we travel up the river. Along the river are small towns and villages. The people wave. Some of the villages have schools and other buildings. We move still deeper into the forest. The villages are getting farther from the river **banks**.

As we travel on, it seems like we are passing back in time. We stop at one village. It is in a clearing in the forest. The guide tells us to follow him and do as he does.

The villagers have lived here for hundreds of years. They live today like they did long ago. All the people in the village share their things. They use blowguns to hunt for food. Darts are tipped with poison from a woody vine.

We see some men coming back from fishing. They do not use fishing poles. Instead, they use a poison made from the barbasco plant. The men pour it into the river. It stuns the fish. Then they wade in and collect the fish.

A villager hunts with a blowgun.

Into the Rain Forest

The rain forest looks like a giant green blanket from the air. But it has layers and each layer is different.

The ground layer is the **forest floor**. It is full of wet leaves. Bugs on the forest floor eat the leaves. We see what looks like a big black animal moving towards us. Our guide tells us that it is really a large group of tiny millipedes.

The next level is the **understory**. Green plants hang down like ropes. Big snakes wind around the branches.

The next level looks like a large umbrella. It is called the **canopy**. Here is where we see parrots flying and spider monkeys swinging on the vines. There are sloths hanging upside down by their three toes.

The top level is called the **emergent level**. Here tall trees stick out. Harpy eagles nest here. They seem to guard the forest.

Sloth

Amazing Plants and Animals

Many strange plants and animals live in the part of the rain forest along the Amazon. We try to spot as many plants and animals as we can.

I notice a horrible smell. It's a plant called rafflesia bloom! It's the biggest flower in the world. Its bloom is closed now because it only opens at night. Its bloom lasts for a full week.

Next, I think I see a lobster's claw, but it's a flower. The guide says there are 450 kinds of this flower here. It looks like lobsters lined up on a tree. These flowers love the hot, damp climate of the rain forest.

Rafflesia bloom

Jaguar

The guide holds up his hand. There is a jaguar. It is the "king" of the Amazon. It is the biggest cat in the forest. This one is sleeping in a tree. We move away quietly.

Suddenly we spot squirrel monkeys. There are about 30 of them. They chatter and swing quickly around. They eat fruit, birds' eggs, and juicy spiders. I'm not afraid of them.

The scorpion does scare me. It is on a tree. The guide points to it. I'm glad I was paying attention. I almost put my hand there! I see an iguana scurry away. Too bad they are so shy. I'd like to see one up close.

Our guide brings us back to the canoe. It is time to make it to the source of the Amazon. That's where the river begins. Our trip is almost over.

The river gets narrower and narrower as we get closer to the source. We are high in the Andes Mountains. At last we reach a small lake called Lake McIntyre. It is the source of the Amazon River. Water from this lake flows down the mountain. Other streams flow into it until it builds to the mighty Amazon that cuts across most of South America.

The Amazon is an amazing river. It holds many secrets. There are still many parts left to explore. There are many more strange plants and animals to see. I'm already planning my next trip. Want to come along?

Glossary

bank	the land along each side of a river
canopy	the level of a rain forest between the understory and the emergent level
current	the flow of water
emergent level	the top level of a rain forest
forest floor	the bottom level, or floor, of a rain forest
mouth	the place where a river empties into a large body of water
plantation	a large farm
port	a place where ships can dock and load and unload goods
rain forest	an area with many tall trees that gets large amounts of rain each year
rapids	parts of a river where the currents are fast
sediment	materials such as the sand, clay, and rock that settle at the bottom of a river
source	the place where a river starts
tributary	a stream that flows into a river
understory	the level of a rain forest between the forest floor and the canopy

Index